The Most Wonderful King

LUKE 19:28 – 24:43

AND

JOHN 12:12 – 20:31

FOR CHILDREN

Written by
Dave Hill

Illustrated by
Betty Wind

ARCH® Books
© 1968 CONCORDIA PUBLISHING HOUSE, ST. LOUIS, MISSOURI

MANUFACTURED IN THE UNITED STATES OF AMERICA
ALL RIGHTS RESERVED

ISBN 0-570-06032-X

Once long ago, when Jesus knew
His time to die had come,
He rode one pleasant Sunday morn
into Jerusalem.

"Our King! Our King!" the people cried
and held their palm leaves high
as Jesus on a donkey's back
came slowly riding by.

Now Jesus was a man of fame
from far-off Galilee.
He healed the sick and raised the dead
and made the blind to see.

"Is He a king?" the people asked,
"*our* king—to set us free?
Will He not fight the Roman rule
and bring us victory?"

But Jesus said, "I've come to bring
God's own Good News to you—
He wants to see you full of joy
in everything you do!

"And I have come to die for you
and take your sins away
so you can live in peace and joy
with lives made new each day."

But certain men—the priests and scribes—
were full of hate and fear.
"The people call this man a king,"
one said. "I've heard them cheer.

"They talk against the Roman king.
He's stirring up a fuss.
Now, if they fight the Romans here,
why—that's the end for us!"

"This cannot be," another cried. "This man must surely die!"

"I vote for death!" a third man cried. "And I!" "And I!" "And I!"

"Then it's agreed," they said as one.
"This man must surely die!"

Now Jesus knew what these men planned.
It made Him want to cry.
But Jesus loved all men so much
that He would gladly die
if by His death all men might know
that God had sent His Son
to die for them and win new lives
of joy for everyone.

He went alone
to talk with God
in dark Gethsemane.
"Your will be done,"
He prayed and wept,
as sad as
He could be.
"Yet if My death
will give
men life,

then, Father,
let it be!"

The soldiers came.
"Are You the man?"

He nodded:
"I am He."

They dragged Him to the prison yard
and threw Him on the ground.
The priests and scribes, who wished Him dead,
stood smirking all around.
They asked of Pilate, "Judge this man."

He asked, "What has He done?"
He says He's king!
He stirs up war!"
the priests all cried as one.
He's in your hands,"
said Pilate then.
You do as you think right."

When people saw
that Jesus would
not lead them out to figh
they turned away.
"He's not *our* king!
So kill Him!
Let Him die!"

"What did you say?" the priests all cried.

They screamed, "Let Jesus die!"

So to the hill called Golgotha
they led the Christ away,
and soldiers nailed Him to a cross
while friends stood near to pray.

And as He hung upon the cross,
a few men heard Him say,
"Forgive them, Father, they don't know
what they have done today."

He prayed to God, and then He died.
His friends were very sad.
The priests and scribes were smiling now.
His death had made them glad.

They put His body in a tomb,
a big stone at the door.
"And that is *that!*" sneered priests and scribes.
"We'll hear of Him no more."

On Sunday morn a few sad friends
came weeping to the tomb.
"The stone was moved," they cried. "He's gone!"
Their hearts were full of gloom.

They looked inside the open grave
and heard two angels say,
"He is not here! HE IS ALIVE!
Go tell the news today."

Soon Jesus came to see His friends
as they hid in a room.
"I've fought with death and won,"
     He said.
"There is no cause for gloom.

"You, Thomas, come and touch My side.
I am alive, you see.
Come, put your finger here
        and touch.
Believe, and follow Me."

Again He came to join two friends
along Emmaus Way.
He stayed to eat, He took the bread,
He raised His eyes to pray.

When Jesus broke the bread for them,
their eyes were opened wide.
They saw that He was Christ the Lord
alive and at their side.

Then on a mount He called His friends
and said, "Go tell all men;
go preach the Word of God's great love
till I shall come again.

"All power is Mine in earth and heaven;
you have no need to fear.
When you're alone and need My help,
I will be standing near."

DEAR PARENTS:

The people at the time of Jesus expected the promised Messiah to come as a mighty king. They looked for Him to sweep away the enemies of God's people and to establish His kingdom with great triumph and glory. When Jesus began to heal the sick and raise the dead, some thought He was the king to overthrow the rule of Roman armies and to restore Israel to the height of power it had enjoyed under King David.

But Jesus did not lead a revolution against the Roman government. He brought love for the lowly, mercy for sinners, and the gracious rule of God to people. Jesus said He would die and rise again for all men. He identified Himself as the Son of God, not a king like David. Before Pilate He confessed that He was a king but that His kingdom was not of this world.

The story is sad because the leaders of the people, the Bible scholars and priests, rejected Jesus, the most wonderful King. They influenced Pontius Pilate, the governor, to order Jesus to the cross. The enemies of Jesus thought they had eliminated Him.

For us this is a happy story. On Friday He carried our sins and died for us on the cross. In rising on Easter morning He broke the power of evil and death.

Jesus is indeed our most wonderful King. We belong to Him. He rules over us now. He is in charge of everything in the world, and we can be sure of His love.

Will you help your child be sure of our Most Wonderful King?

THE EDITOR